LINDA C. BROWN

TESTIMONIALS
Triumph in Jesus

iUniverse LLC
Bloomington

TESTIMONIALS
TRIUMPH IN JESUS

Scripture quotations marked KJV are from the Holy Bible, King James Version (Authorized Version). First published in 1611. Quoted from the KJV Classic Reference Bible, Copyright © 1983 by The Zondervan Corporation.

iUniverse books may be ordered through booksellers or by contacting:

iUniverse LLC
1663 Liberty Drive
Bloomington, IN 47403
www.iuniverse.com
1-800-Authors (1-800-288-4677)

ISBN: 978-1-4917-2766-9 (sc)
ISBN: 978-1-4917-2767-6 (hc)
ISBN: 978-1-4917-2768-3 (e)

Printed in the United States of America.

iUniverse rev. date: 03/31/2014

Dedication

Helen Ruth Brown

With love and remembrance of my late mother, Helen Ruth Brown, the book *Linda C. Brown, Testimonials* is dedicated in memory of her, whom I love and will cherish for the rest of my life.

I appreciate her teachings of good morals, values, and responsibilities that were instrumental to survive in life. She worked hard and long to make sure our everyday needs were met. She knew the Lord who strengthened her to be strong and courageous when confronted with opposition.

I have a great admiration for her inner natural beauty. My mother was always good-hearted, cheerful, harmonious, and the family comedian as she could always make us laugh. Amazingly, her spirit is alive, felt, and seen in my siblings as well as her sisters today.

As a child, I would wait and watch for her to walk across the bridge from a hard day's work. When I would see her, the neighborhood could hear the greeting from me to her.

My mom is in heaven rejoicing with the Lord; I will see her again.

Introduction

Like most loyal, pecan-loving Southerners, my sister, Vivian Brown, and I had a taste for some fresh Southern pecans from John's Grocery, which was one block from our home in Columbia, South Carolina. Although we had the taste, we did not have the money. So, we got creative and planned how we could get the pecans. The plan was for me to entertain the store owner, Mr. John Green, while my sister got the pecans from the huge, oak wood barrel located in the rear of the store, which she successfully did. Once Vivian came toward the front of the store and stood next to me with the hidden pecans, I hastily ended the conversation with Mr. Green as I knew our "mission was accomplished." We had succeeded in our mission to steal the pecans and suffice our taste for Southern pecans that day. Enjoying the crunchy taste of the pecans, Vivian and I talked about how masterfully we executed the plan to steal them. We did not realize my aunt, Bonnie, overheard our conversation and told on us. So, as we were sitting under the shady pine tree, eating our pecans, the next thing we knew, my grandfather was yelling, "Get in the house now!" My aunt had told my grandfather we stole the pecans, and needless to say, my grandfather also sufficed our taste that day for a life lesson in morals and values. He whipped us—and not with holy hands, I might add!

As I flash back on this life lesson and reflect on God's Word in Proverbs 22:15, "Foolishness is bound in the heart of a child; but the rod of correction shall drive it far from him," I am thankful to my granddaddy who corrected me, but always with love. As I was receiving the punishment, my granddaddy would ask and answer his question saying, "I told you not to leave this house while I'm at work . . . didn't I . . . didn't I?" While family love was "tough love," it was loaded with morals and values that positively impacted my life.

Neither my mother nor my grandfather knew the Lord's plan for my life, but their love for God played a role in that plan. God's plan included moving me from working in an hourly, wage-paying movie theater job to a 30-year salary-paying career with the federal government. God's plan included my overcoming insensitivities from teachers in elementary school to winning Most Popular Student in high school. While God's plan was not for me to have a child out of wedlock, I repented of my sin, and He blessed me enormously as a single parent . . . This book will share with you the purpose and plan God has for me and the foundation that fosters the *Linda C. Brown Testimonials.*

"The righteous perisheth, and no man layeth it to heart: and merciful men are taken away, none considering that the righteous is taken away from the evil to come . . ." Isaiah 57:1.

Testimonial

"My Childhood"

Adversity, death, heartache, pain, and sorrows are consequences of living in a fallen world because of sin. At the age of 10, my family and I experienced these elements of the world. We trusted the Lord who comforts us in all our afflictions. November 13, 1961, was a memorable night the seed of trust and faith was instilled into my soul.

My granddaddy was a family-oriented man. He was employed as a gardener during the day and a janitor at night. One of his employers gave him a wooden stove, and he did not hesitate to install it. We were ecstatic about our new stove. It surely was an upgrade from the previous one. We observed it generated heat much faster and hotter than the old stove. It was a very cold winter night as we were snuggled around, enjoying the warmth it produced. My grandmother decided she was going to make full use of this stove by making chicken and dumplings. She was a great cook. After we ate our chicken and dumplings, we were warm, ecstatic, and full.

Two hours later, my mother and aunts were preparing for a club meeting to be held at our home. My mom instructed me to entertain the younger ones until the meeting adjourned. I am the eldest of my siblings and 10 first cousins. Our entertainment was playing school and storytelling. My twin cousins approached the room, desiring to join us. They were toddlers. I knew they could not remain silent and attentive. Jack and Jackie, the twins, were too young to be knowledgeable and aware to have participated. I urged them to go downstairs to our grandparents' bedroom.

Approximately 20 minutes after the twins were gone; I heard an explosive noise that shook the house. I immediately ushered my siblings and cousins out of the house. As we were rushing out, I heard despairing cries and screams of agony coming from my grandparents' bedroom. I started crying because I realized something tragic had occurred.

The whole community was there to assist us, and the rescue team was on the way. I was determined to go back inside to see what happened. I ran into my grandparents' bedroom and cried, "Oh, Lord, no!" I was horrified and heartbroken to find that the wooden stove had exploded, killing 2-year-old Jackie from head trauma—literally knocking her brains out. Her twin brother, Jack, was lying next to her with a cracked skull. My sister was burned badly on her back. My grandmother was an amputee due to diabetes and was injured on her one remaining leg. My mother was leaving the room when the stove exploded. She looked back to see what had happened, and hot liquid splashed on her face.

I felt guilty about Jackie's death because I told them to go downstairs to that room. My granddaddy felt guilty and responsible for this fatality because he installed the stove earlier that day. No instructions were given, and he had no insight that the stove would cause destruction to our home and our lives.

There was an enormous outpour of support from neighbors, friends, and people throughout the city, embracing us with love and compassion. This type of response was soothing, comforting to our heartache during our time of bereavement as our family was very appreciative and grateful for the support and generosity received.

When adversity strikes, it's an opportunity to demonstrate the characteristics of God. We know little Jackie's soul is with the Lord. He is our comforter, Savior, and His Word is true.

Jack, the surviving twin, presently lives and works in Los Angeles, California. His lovely wife Bridgette is a court reporter for the state of California. Jack and Bridgette have a beautiful daughter, Takena, who is currently in high school. Years later, Jack was blessed with another sister, the adorable Mrs. Ava Jenkins.

My sister Sarah, also a survivor from the explosion, is employed with Richland County Healthcare, living in Columbia, South Carolina. She is a very softhearted person. If she knows of a family member that's ill, she will visit that individual. She will bring a supply of groceries to last for a week during that visit. Sarah will also serve the individual breakfast in bed. Sarah not only feels compassion, she shows it. Trust me, though, her kindness is not weakness. One night after a long day of hard work, Sarah cracked her window to get some fresh air. This was to help unwind her body to be alert for work the next day. As she lay down and began to sleep, she was quickly awakened by an intruder who entered her home through a window. She awoke to her amazement to see him standing at the foot of her bed. She grabbed her bat to go to battle; he made tracks out of the same window he came in.

God loves and uses people that are not qualified by man's earthly standards. "For my thoughts are not your thoughts, neither are your ways my ways, saith the Lord," Isaiah 55:8.

Testimonial

"Grammar School"

The first day of grammar school I learned my first lesson: "All men are created equally but not treated equally." I observed most teachers embraced students that were from families of prominence. While I did not know what *prominence* meant at the time, I knew the behavior toward me was wrong. I later realized as an innocent child, one can feel ostracized. My family background was not one of money, prestige, or worldly standards as demonstrated by this particular school.

I remember we had a program one night during my fourth-grade school year. Before the principal gave his closing remarks, he ordered all lights turned off except his selected few. He wanted the lights to remain sunny and bright on his chosen ones. The chosen ones were always separated from the regular folk like me.

I recall a few teachers who showed humanity. My second-grade teacher, Mrs. Myers, exercised the fruits of the Spirit: love, joy, gentleness, and goodness. In her classroom, I had a front-row seat. She spent quality time to teach each student. I participated in all the classroom activities. At the end of the school term, Mrs. Myers expressed approval and admiration for work and effort that each student put forth.

Later in life, I learned that money cannot buy everything. All the money in the world cannot buy one soul to heaven. It can buy a house, but not a home. It cannot buy love. After Mrs. Myers's classroom, I experienced the equality method of teaching students. This behavior from teachers toward their favorites continued on from second grade until I graduated from elementary school in the sixth grade. I was glad to leave grammar school as in junior high and high school, I was treated fairly; and that, I loved.

"Oh that men would praise the Lord for his goodness,

and for his wonderful works to the children of men!"

Psalm 107:8

Testimonial

"High School"

Booker T. Washington High School (BTW) was historical and the bum! The faculty and student body were cool. BTW High School excelled in academics and extracurricular activities. The school had a reputation for winning and achievement. Scholarships were accomplished in scholastics and athletics. A former classmate, Barnette Jackson, played professional basketball for the Chicago Bulls. Many BTW graduates furthered their education to attain their occupational goals and are very successful to date.

I know the Holy Spirit led me to BTW. I've always loved people, conversing, laughter, and joy. AT BTW, I enjoyed the people as they were wholesome and down-to-earth. This made my learning experience insightful and fun.

The school band, "The Marching 100," was also competitive. Whenever they performed, they knew how to close it out. My childhood friend, Tracy, was on the majorette squad and I, too, desired to become a BTW majorette. She taught me how to twirl a baton. Faith without works is dead, so I spent hours at my home practicing. I prayed to the Lord to give me the ability to qualify for the tryouts. A few days after the tryouts, the names of the selected majorettes were posted on a board in the school gym. Tracy saw the list and rushed to tell me that I had made the majorette squad. I was shocked and said, "Thank you, Lord."

After I made the majorette squad, I was blessed with other achievements. When the Lord blesses you, Satan gets mad. Making the high school majorette squad was a lesson in self-esteem. As I reflect on a memorable incident during my high school years, I remember feeling low self-esteem as we had gathered for a class meeting in the school auditorium. While we waited for the guest speaker, a student suggested that we elect our junior class officers. My name was called to be nominated for the office of secretary. Yet, I was stunned at the reaction of my teacher who was facilitating the election. Without hesitation, she immediately let out a loud moan of discontentment, saying, "Oh no, not Linda C. Brown; she does not take notes in my class." I felt so humiliated, embarrassed, and filled with shame. I commented to myself, "No, she didn't say that!" Maybe I was not worthy. Maybe I was not someone who should feel good about me. Was she right?

At that moment, I had no self-esteem. But the class officers' election continued and several of the football players stood up in my defense. They shouted, "What's wrong with Linda C. Brown? This is *our* junior class, and she's who we want to elect, no matter what you say." Now I was really confused about myself and my ability to perform this task. *Was I even worthy?* My teacher didn't feel that I was worthy. What a negative impact she was having on me.

As each nominee's name was called for the office of secretary, there were few responses for my competitors. When my name was called, the response was overwhelming. Almost the entire auditorium stood up, clapping and roaring my name. It was an overwhelming majority that voted for me. It was truly amazing. Yes, I was the "people's choice," and yes, the "people" spoke and felt I was worthy.

As my confidence improved, I felt so much better about myself. I was already a majorette and had previously run track in middle school. I was voted "Miss Junior" by my classmates. And even more gratifying, when we became seniors, they voted me as "Most Popular" and "Most Witty" in our Senior Class Superlatives.

So it is, God loves all of us and feels that we are all worthy. He wants us to feel good about ourselves as His children. He has a plan for us all. Never let man pull your self-esteem down, but trust in God who is always in control.

"Repent ye therefore, and be converted, that your sins may be blotted out, when the times of refreshing shall come from the presence of the Lord," Acts 3:19.

Testimonial

"Repentance of Sins"

Raised in the church, I knew the Lord at an early age. However, it was not until I was 21 that I really understood God's salvation plan for me. Once we are Christians we will find ourselves having to repent about many things, with God always ready to forgive.

God forgave me during a time when I had a beautiful daughter out of wedlock and was not mature in my spiritual growth or walk with the Lord. However, I repented of that sin and was forgiven by the Lord. I had hopes of a marriage with my daughter's dad. I learned later that this was not the Lord's will. I was hurt because of disobedience to the Word of God. I prayed for healing of my womb; and in his timing, I was healed. "If we say that we have not sinned, we make him a liar, and his word is not in us," 1 John 1:10.

It was Jesus Christ who paid our sin debt on the cross. He came and was beaten, crucified, humiliated, and died a shameful death. But, it was early Sunday morning when He arose with all power in His hands.

Jesus suffered so that we can have salvation eternally. Have you professed with your mouth and believed in your heart that He is the Son of God and that He died for our sins? If yes, praise the Lord! If no, I pray for your heart to be touched by the Holy Spirit to accept Jesus Christ as your Lord and Savior as you read this book.

The worst thing that can happen to mankind is to die and go to hell. It's not God's will for anybody to spend eternity in hell. Hell was not made for man, but if you refuse to accept Christ as your Savior, that will be your eternal destiny.

Jesus said that He came to save the lost. "They that are whole have no need of the physician, but they that are sick: I came not to call the righteous, but sinners to repentance," Mark 2:17.

Allow today to become the day of your salvation. Repent of your sins, accept Christ as your Lord and Savior, and be converted. Be ready at all times for Christ's return. Don't put off today for tomorrow; tomorrow may be too late. Jesus said, "And this know, that if the goodman of the house had known what hour the thief would come, he would have watched, and not have suffered his house to be broken through. Be ye therefore ready also: for the Son of man cometh at an hour when ye think not," Luke 12:39-40.

"By faith Noah, being warned of God of things not seen as yet, moved with fear, prepared an ark to the saving of his house; by the which he condemned the world, and became heir of the righteousness which is by faith," Hebrews 11:7.

Testimonial

"Necessity of Faith"

I heard the voice of the Lord to move to Los Angeles, California, where my blessings were. He told Abraham to leave his country and kindred and go to a land where he would be blessed. Abraham obeyed, and so did I. I moved 3,000 miles from my original home in Columbia, South Carolina. I stepped out in faith, trusting the Lord for His promises of things not seen yet.

The move to Los Angeles from my hometown and familiar surroundings to a new place and environment was not easy. It was very challenging and a major adjustment. I tremendously missed my daughter, family, and their support. Moving was a necessity for me to obey the Lord and to give my toddler child a better education and quality of life that I didn't have for myself as a child. I was thankful that my daughter's paternal grandaunt and—uncle kept her in my hometown for approximately 6 months while I made the move to Los Angeles. I wanted to be situated with a job, an apartment, and car before having my daughter join me in California.

Everything was a hustle, and I couldn't take my eyes off of the prize. I had to stay focused and give faith a chance. I reunited with a half sister, who I barely knew, living in the Los Angeles area. I tried living with her temporarily until I got my own place. Her lifestyle was not one that I wanted my child exposed to as our morals and values were opposites.

It was such a difficult challenge to obtain a job with benefits. I also was challenged finding a job on a nearby bus line. So, my next goal was to get a car and an apartment.

Giving all praise and glory to the Lord God Almighty, all the goals that I set were fulfilled. A job with benefits on a nearby bus line, an apartment, a car, and my reunion with my daughter were all realized. I was 28 years old, and my daughter was 2 years old when we settled in the Los Angeles, California, area.

"For as the body without the spirit is dead, so faith without works is dead also," James 2:26.

Testimonial

"Faith and Works"

This scripture convicted me to work with the homeless. I planned a small gathering of 10 people to have dinner at my home and to socialize. My coworker, Mr. Lee, owned a restaurant, so I decided to have everything catered for 15 people. Disappointingly, however, only one person showed up. Now I had all this food and nobody to eat it. I was full just from looking at so much food, so I decided to get rid of it by throwing it in the trash bin.

After I threw the food away, I heard the Lord's voice so clearly, saying, "You were wrong." He said that there are hungry people in the downtown area on skid row who would have been glad to have eaten that food.

I felt so guilty. I repented of doing wrong and made a deal to make up for it. Two weeks later, I ordered the same food, along with takeout containers, for 20 to 25 people. I met Mr. Lee, the caterer, on the parking lot at work, and he transferred seven large pans of meats and vegetables to my car. I stopped at the store, picked up some sodas, and headed downtown to skid row to share the food with the homeless people in the area.

Before leaving the parking lot, I had a little talk with the Lord. I said, "Lord, I am taking all this food downtown to skid row to feed the homeless to make good of my earlier wrongdoing. I do not want to bring back one piece of this food." I heard the Lord so clearly. He said, "I promise, you will not."

I arrived downtown to distribute the food. I parked my car on the street, got out, and began thinking, "OK, Lord, what's next?" I observed my surroundings in preparation to start the distribution. A man was walking down the sidewalk near me, so I asked him if he wanted some food. He said, "Yes." I opened my car doors, fixed him a container, and the rest was history. I told him that I wanted to feed other people until it was all gone. He yelled, "Hey, everybody, we got food over here. Come and get it!" I looked up. About a hundred people were lined up to eat. He and a lady helped me to prepare and distribute the containers to the individuals.

After all the food was gone, there remained about 20 people in line who didn't get food to eat. I apologized to them for not having enough food for everyone. I was amazed! The Lord promised me I would not bring back any food, and I didn't. Even the crumbs in the containers were eaten.

When you use your time and talent to help people, you will fulfill the Lord's will and enjoy it. This is how I started to work weekly with a local church homeless ministry, Love LA, evangelizing the Word and distributing food at the end of the service. "It is written, that man shall not live by bread alone, but every word of God," Luke 4:4.

Every Sunday from 3:00 to 5:00 P.M., I participated in the homeless ministry church services, and at the end of the service, the ministry of feeding was done. I love to interact and fellowship with people about the Lord's Word. In addition to the feeding, I was assigned to take prayer requests and pray if asked. It was an opportunity to witness about the goodness of our Lord and Savior, Jesus Christ. "If a brother or sister be naked, and destitute of daily food, And one of you say unto them, Depart in peace, be ye warmed and filled; notwithstanding ye give them not those things which are needful to the body; what doth it profit?" James 2:15-16

I continued working for years on Sundays with the homeless, and it was always heartwarming. Many days I drove away crying. I saw their sorrows, brokenness, and bondage to the flesh. I witnessed that Jesus was the solution to their everyday needs and struggles. Jesus said, "Consider the ravens: for they neither sow nor reap; which neither have storehouse nor barn; and God feedeth them: how much more are ye better than the fowls?" Luke 12:24

Some people from the congregation give testimonials of salvation, deliverance from alcohol and drug abuse, finding jobs and housing. God is a God of grace, mercy, restoration, protection, and salvation.

The church I currently attend and many other churches have a homeless ministry that serves skid row. "Love LA" was the ministry I collaborated with on this project.

Testimonial

"Faith and Works"

I was raised in a small town where everybody knew everybody. The town was safe, so at the age of 13, I would visit elderly people and run errands for them. Around 1993, I started visiting a convalescent home to fellowship with the elderly residents in the facility. Prior to my visits, I pray for the Holy Spirit to lead and tell me what to say. Whatever the Lord puts on my heart to say or to do, I follow. I pray, read scriptures, sing, and shout, giving God the glory!

Sometimes I am led to listen to what is on the hearts of the saints I visit in the home. They are well seasoned with God's Word and love to tell stories of their upbringing, which, in turn, witnesses to me. I always enjoy the visits! One of these saints shared with me how she used to get out of bed 5:00 A.M. every morning and do chores before attending school. On Sundays, everybody in her household attended church; it was not optional, but mandated to fellowship in God's Word every Sunday. During church service, if you misbehaved in church, you knew you would have an "after session" with your parent when you got home that was not a happy occasion.

Some of the residents were not competent because of illnesses or very old age, yet they remember certain verses from the Bible. Jesus said that heaven and earth shall pass away, but His Word will not.

We are all equipped with God-given spiritual gifts to enhance the lives of others. Jesus said that when you have done unto the least of these, you have done unto Him also.

"And he bearing his cross went forth into a place called the place of a skull, which is called in the Hebrew Golgotha," John 19:17.

Testimonial

"Image of the Cross"

I witnessed a cross, which appeared unexpectedly at a couple's home. This cross was phenomenal! The mass of people, astonished by the appearance of the cross on Third Street, strongly desired to see a close-up view. The resident of the home, Pam, a middle-aged woman, established a system for the general public to view the cross by appointments only. When I finally was able to speak with this resident owner, she explained that people who were sick prayed as they viewed the cross and were healed of their sickness.

Additionally, she explained how she discovered the cross outside of the window. The woman's sister had visited and observed a bright light coming from the living room. They went to examine the bright light and saw a huge cross through the window. Personally, I've never seen any visual so awesome, either before or after this viewing of the cross, shining like the bright sun.

She continued to tell me a little concerning her childhood. She has always had a relationship with Christ. As a child, she imagined sharing her tea with Jesus. Her dad was a humanitarian; he provided food and shelter for other people until they had the ability to live independently. Her father's act of generosity influenced Pam's action of helping people through the viewing of the cross, something she always wanted to do.

Jesus said: "If ye abide in me, and my words abide in you, ye shall ask what ye will, and it shall be done unto you," John 15:7.

Testimonial

"Blessings"

Once I became impregnated with abiding in God's Word, I began to birth blessings from God, coming and going. I was blessed with employment at the United States Postal Service (USPS), a prayer that was answered, yielding an immense impact on my livelihood. It was the pivotal point in my life and the bridge to upward mobility. My daughter and I were now enjoying a better quality of life. She was 7 years old when I began employment with USPS. Now, I was happy to be able to afford an excellent education for my daughter. My career with the USPS enhanced my business maturity to become more independent, responsible, accountable, and knowledgeable. My colleagues were of diverse backgrounds from various regions around the world. I always respected diversity and enjoyed working with people from other places. In fact, one of my colleagues invited me to attend a church where she fellowshipped. This invitation resulted in a 15-year membership, under the anointed Bishop Kenneth C. Ulmer, senior pastor and teacher of Faithful Central Bible Church, located in Inglewood, California.

I praise Jesus for His goodness in blessing me with the opportunity to work 29 years and counting for the United States governmental agency. This job has kept food on the table in our home, a roof over our heads, clothes on our backs, and more blessings. Doors of opportunities were opening up for me like never before.

Blessings from Jesus started flowing one after another. I did not anticipate becoming an entrepreneur. I purchased a triplex, with a two-bedroom unit in each section, and became a landlord. I was elated!

Home is where you want comfort while feeling secure and safe. A home environment that is healthy is best. This triplex building was purchased "as is." I bought the triplex unit with plans of doing a makeover because I purchased it at a good price and I saw huge potential with the unit. Each of the three units was occupied when I purchased the property.

I met with the tenants to hear and acknowledge their concerns. I expressed my appreciation and assured each of the tenants his or her home would be upgraded. I asked that they be patient with the process and give me the time to create a plan for remodeling the units.

The handyman I contracted organized a crew to help with the makeover. The crew painted, replaced old windows, and laid new plush carpet. When the project was completed, there was jubilation and celebration heard throughout the newly remodeled triplex unit.

My philosophy was to always timely respond to a tenant's needs. I preferred to maintain the long-term tenants by keeping rents affordable, not raising them each year. This was the reward for loyal tenants who always paid their rent on time. Rather than evict tenants for monetary gain, tenants were acknowledged with facility updates and remodeling, not doubling the rent.

Eviction is a slow process, not in the immediate favor of landlords. Until the eviction notices are served, tenants can live rent-free for months and the owner does not get paid any money during the eviction process. I was blessed to only have to serve one eviction notice during this 10-year landlord experience.

I thank and praise the Lord for the triplex property. It was a financial blessing and a spiritual and maturity growth period for me. It was an opportunity to make a difference in people's lives. I realized this was a business purchase, but I also considered the human element of people's living conditions. Tenants deserve comfort and decency in exchange for rent. Maintaining ownership of this property blessed me with the necessities of my family life, and the assurance of my spiritual faith in God. His plan was for me to become a landlord by allowing me to first become a tenant. He groomed me to become a mature businesswoman and to treat tenants with love, compassion, and respect.

I recall one of the tenants was a lady with four young children in desperate need of a home for her family. She had a Section VIII certificate that required occupancy within 5 days or it would have expired. God allowed me in this landlord position for such a time as this because when I interviewed her, my heart was deeply touched. I had remembered when I moved to Los Angeles as a single mom, my immediate concern was that

I needed a home for my daughter and me. God had made a way for us and now He had made a way for this lady to be blessed with housing, thus preventing her Section VIII certificate from expiring.

Sometimes Christ allows us to go through hardships to teach, mold, and groom us for His plan in our lives. When we are strengthened and see a sister or brother down and out, we must lift them up. Tell them, "I know what you are going through; I've been there." Testify how God brought you from "there" and that He will do the same for them.

Testimonial

"Blessings"

My daughter was growing and now was a preteen, so we needed more room. This was 2 years after the first rental property purchase. So, a need and motivation entered my mind with the thought to purchase again.

Acting on faith, I threw away old furniture, clothes, and whatever I didn't want to carry into my new home. I cleaned out all the closets.

One year later, we moved into a two-bedroom condo on the borderline of Culver City, California. The positive cash overflow from the rental property units was paying most of the note for my two-bedroom condo. I thanked God as these were answered prayers and blessings, indeed!

Jesus showed me another truth of His marvelous kindness. When you abide in His Word, He promises to answer your prayers. Blessings come in different ways of life: joy, peace, love, and health. Put Christ first in your life always and triumph over the adversary, Satan.

I was trapped in an elevator along with two other people at work for about 5 minutes one day. Some of my colleagues began to panic, but the

Holy Spirit told me to pray. I prayed in the name of Jesus and the door opened!

I know a person that wanted deliverance from alcohol addiction. We prayed a prayer in Jesus' name and that person was healed by Jesus and is now alcohol-free for the past 10 years.

Make Jesus your Lord and Savior today. He will heal you and set you free.

"And Joseph said unto Pharaoh, The dream of Pharaoh is one: God hath shewed Pharaoh what he is about to do," Genesis 41:25.

Testimonial

"Prophetic Dreams Fulfilled"

God has made Himself known to me through dreams also. He has healed, warned, delivered, revealed, and prepared me for future events as I slept. I love sharing inspirational dreams that unbelievably come to past.

One night I dreamed I was visiting the sick and shut-ins at a hospital. A lady told me Jesus was downstairs. I said, "Oh, I want to see Jesus!" The next moment, I saw Jesus smiling as He walked toward me. When He approached me I said, "Jesus I've wanted to see you." He said, "I know." We then looked eye to eye. He put His hands on my shoulders and started praying in tongues to His Father. I didn't understand what He prayed, but when He finished, He said, "By my stripes you are healed."

I woke up that morning in my home praising, shouting, and thanking the Lord for the healing. While I was not aware of any illness, I believed I was healed and anyone else to whom this Word of God applied. I later believed this word from God was for my daughter.

Warned in a dream, my life was saved. One night I dreamed I was in a doctor's office. The doctor told me I was going to die soon. I responded,

"No, I'm not." He said, "Yes, you are. If you don't stop eating red meat, you are going to die." I said, "I will stop eating red meat." I have not eaten any red meat since that dream and am still alive, standing on faith in Jesus' name. Witnessing the loss of my loved ones at an early age to diabetes, I decided to change my diet even more. I do not eat pork. I only eat the fish in the water that have fins and scales as well as chicken and turkey.

God is a God who can heal and will warn us, even in dreams, because He loves and cares for us immensely. God is omnipotent!

Testimonial

"Prophetic Dreams Fulfilled"

I dreamed I was in New York City, a place I had never visited although some of my family was living there, including my sister who had made New York City her home after becoming an adult. In the dream I was carefully observing the city from a window, and the time period was 2 years prior to my actual visit to New York.

In her later years, my sister became diabetic and had to undergo dialysis treatment three times a week. One day she had complications from the treatment and was hospitalized. Whenever we talked from her sick bed, she was upset. I knew she needed me for help and support during her troubled times.

I wanted to be there in New York City for my sister, but was apprehensive about airplanes due to my fear of flying. I flew several times, but could never relax during the flights. My sister's hospitalization occurred 2 months after 9/11, which made it worse for me to consider flying to any city, much less to my sister's home in New York.

I prayed in the name of Jesus. I needed and wanted to go there as my sister had been in the hospital for a month and was very depressed. It was fear that prevented me from traveling to be with my sister.

The Almighty God answered my prayers and prevailed, however. He first reminded me of the dream of being in New York 2 years prior to my sister's medical complications. Second, whatever God promises, He is able to perform. He instructed me to go see my sister and carry some anointing oil and the Bible.

I made arrangements to take a 2-week vacation from work and flew to New York City. When I arrived in my sister's room, we greeted and hugged each other. After the greeting, I turned and observed the city from the window, which was exactly the same as the vision in my dream.

That evening, my sister's soul was fed with God's Word and her body was anointed for healing to relieve tension. That night she slept like a baby, snoring so loud, I could not sleep. Yet, I was so happy to see my sister relaxed; it didn't matter about my sleep. After fasting and praying, my sister was discharged from the hospital the same week I arrived. God's prophesy and promise was fulfilled.

God, who created the heaven and the earth, delivered me from the fear of flying. I had an out-of-body experience as I slept. During this dream, my spirit was floating in the air, surrounded by airplanes. After this happened, I've never feared flying on an airplane anymore. Praise ye the Lord for deliverance!

I love traveling now as during the flight, I read the Word, listen to my spiritual tapes, and eat snacks. There was one flight which I slept through the entire time and got some solid rest. My only memory was getting on and off of the airplane. Normally I am awake, so when the airplane touches down, I thank and praise God for a safe flight.

After years of a childless marriage, my cousins trusted the Lord for a child after having prior difficulties with two unsuccessful pregnancies. The Lord showed me a dream, that the wife had a full-term pregnancy that was successful. This was good news for the couple and the answer to their prayers.

Two years later, the dream came to pass. The wife had a full-term pregnancy and normal birth. Their daughter is a beautiful, healthy 16 year old today.

Testimonial

"Prophetic Dreams Fulfilled"

I can identify my true dreams from the untrue dreams that will come to pass. When the vision is clear, I remember the details of it when I awake. I know it is true. Only God can predict the future; He prepares us through visions.

My sister, Audrey, who is stylish and wholehearted, also has visions. One day, while she was at the mirror, over her shoulder appeared a vision of a friend. Moments later, she learned of her friend's death, who had actually been murdered in real life.

The Lord revealed a coworker was killed by a gun in a dream to me. The next morning, I was terrified. I said, "O Lord, no, please don't allow this to happen." Thirteen years later, sadly to say, the same vision from my dream of David, the coworker, came to pass. As I was preparing for work, it was announced on television: David was shot and killed by gunfire. Then I remembered what I had dreamed. A week before David's death, my auntie had a premonition concerning it as well. She dreamed David and my mother were having a conversation in her kitchen. My auntie and

I could not figure out what the dream meant, because my mother had been deceased for 25 years. When she told me about the dream and gave a description of the person in her dream, I knew it was David.

I dreamed I was standing at a casket viewing the body of a young person but could not see a face. About 5 years later, I had another dream of a black handgun in an environment that I was trying to get away from. Hours later, I got the bad news: my nephew was shot and killed in New York, a day before his twenty-sixth birthday.

My nephew's son was 9 years old when his father was gunned down. Fourteen years later, I am proud to share the news that my nephew's son joined the New York Police Department in the summer of 2013 and is taking a stand to fight against crime. He is now 23 years old. I pray for him and all police officers who risk their lives to make this world a safer place to live.

Testimonial

"Prophetic Dreams Fulfilled"

I dreamed a celebrity named Scott visited our home in Los Angeles, California. While the dream was delightful to have a famous person in my home, it was unusual as the setting was a marriage scene. I woke up and said to myself, "Lord, I know you are awesome, but I'm old enough to be his mother." Then I said, "A celebrity in my home is only a dream."

Two years later, my daughter was at a mall in Beverly Hills. Walking around a corner, she physically bumped into this same celebrity who had been in my dream. He asked for her phone number and they exchanged numbers. The following week he visited my daughter in our home and they dated for a period of time. Here is yet another vision that came to pass!

What are your dreams? Dream big and trust the Lord to bring it to pass. You have the assurance of receiving what you want, according to God's Word. Jesus said, "Verily, verily, I say unto you, He that believeth on me, the works that I do shall he do also; and greater works than these shall he do; because I go unto my Father. If ye shall ask any thing in my name, I will do it," John 14:12, 14.

My daughter Tanta and I were living in our two-bedroom condominium home when I saw a large spacious house in my dream. This same dream was repeated a few times that year. This beautiful home was only imaginative for me. But through God, all things are possible, and He made it possible. Fifteen years later, this dream home came to pass. It is a blessing! This five-bedroom, spacious upstairs and downstairs brand-new brick home is my blessing, my dream home from God!

Located in my hometown of Columbia, South Carolina, I now have a vacation home away from my home in Los Angeles. When vacationing at my home in Columbia, I meditate on my deck, absorbing all of God's creations: beautiful scenery, animals, and more! The tranquility from viewing giant green trees and listening to birds chirping from tree to tree gives a peace that surpasses all.

"Know ye not that they which run in a race run all, but one receiveth the prize? So run, that ye may obtain," 1 Corinthians 9:24.

Testimonial

"Running the Race"

Tanta, my daughter, grew up as a healthy person. She never experienced a major illness, only common colds once in a while. I was thankful to the Lord for her good health.

When she became a young adult, she began to experience headaches frequently. I massaged her head in hopes of relieving stress and tension. This worked for a few days, but the pain reoccurred later. The headaches became severe and unbearable one day, so we immediately sought and found a neurologist who ordered X-rays to be taken and scheduled a follow-up office visit for the diagnosis. Driving home from the x-ray facility, I noticed Tanta's sad look. I tried to console her, saying, "Not to worry, everything is going to be all right." She said, "No, Momma, the technician told me something large is near my brain." I was devastated. I wanted to go back to tell that technician what his job duties were. He had no right to say what he saw, because he was an x-ray technician and not a physician.

The next day as I was preparing for church, I observed Tanta depressed again. She was young and not used to dealing with major illnesses of any kind. Uncertain if this "something large near my brain" could be life-threatening was on her mind, I, too, was feeling hurt and concerned but had to trust the Lord for the outcome.

Tanta didn't plan to fellowship with me at church because she was worried. I said, "In the name of Jesus, I will not miss praising the Lord at church to have a pity party at home. I'm going to thank Him today by faith you are healed. We are children of the Lord. He hears and answers our prayers." After this short talk, Tanta's spirits were lifted, and she fellowshipped with me. Praise the Lord!

At the altar call, the deacon prayed and said, "Someone here just found out they have cancer. But the Lord is with you."

The next day, Monday, we carried the x-rays to the doctor and waited for the full diagnosis. Tanta and I were seated when he approached us and said, "I have bad news. You have a large brain tumor." Our hearts ached. This was confirmation of what we did *not* want to hear. We later found out it was cancerous. But the tumor was operable because it was located outside of the brain. God is good!

Before an athlete runs in a race, he goes through a preparation period. He has a coach to train and instruct him or her on what foods to eat and the number of hours of exercise needed. These are necessities to get the body in shape for wholesomeness to achieve the goal.

This was a serious, major life-or-death race Tanta had to run, because the adversary was cancer. Even with all the love I had for her, yet, I had no power to heal her. I knew Jesus had all the power, and I knew Jesus could heal Tanta. His Word teaches: "Then Jesus answering said unto them, Go your way, and tell John what things ye have seen and heard; how that the blind see, the lame walk, the lepers are cleansed, the deaf hear, the dead are raised, to the poor the gospel is preached," Luke 7:22.

Have faith in God. What things you desire, believe in your heart, not to doubt, and they shall come to pass. I fasted and prayed for the Lord to heal my only child and to strengthen both of us to endure this race.

I was Tanta's coach, a race with Jesus in mind. The Holy Word was my coaching tool for the preparation period. I prepared her for the challenges and hardships that she would be subjected to. She had to run with faith, patience, long-suffering, and endurance. "It is time for the race to start," I told my daughter at that moment.

The week of the neurosurgery, her hair was shaved from her head. Hours before Tanta's surgery, the Lord revealed in my dream her face with her hair down on her shoulders. What a blessing and comfort from God, letting me know everything was going to be all right. The surgery was successful! Praise the Lord! Tanta was halfway to the finish line.

The treatments were the hardships. I coached her from the sidelines to press on toward the mark. "You will make it through Christ who strengthens you." Once the treatments were over, Tanta got the victory! She fought the fight, finished the race, and kept the faith through it all! She did not run or labor in vain. She has been healed from cancer for 8 years now. "But thanks to God, which giveth us the victory through our Lord Jesus Christ," 1 Corinthians 15:57.

EMPLOYEE APPRECIATION SUPERVISOR RECOGNITION FORM

Date: 9/21/2010

Print name of SUPERVISOR submitting form: **Rhonda Cannon**

Print name of employee who you would like to recognize for an appreciation award: **Linda Brown**

Tour: 3

Please print reason you feel employee should receive a recognition award.

I recommend import express clerk Linda Brown for an appreciation award. She has a very strong work ethic and is always willing and able to perform any assigned task. She is dedicated and committed to the USPS and demonstrates these traits on a daily basis.

Job Performance Recognition

Dream Home: that came to pass

Jack—Survivor of stove explosion with wife & daughter

Deaconess Evelyn Mitchell, Aunt

Late Deacon Eddie Mitchell, Sr., Uncle

Sister Audrey Bridgett, Visionary

Auntie Nellie Brown, Humanitarian

MISS JUNIOR
Linda Carol Brown

Photograph from High School Year Book

Linda Carol Brown, Miss Junior for 1968-69, is witty, popular, and vivacious. The daughter of Mrs. Helen Brown, Linda is secretary of the junior class is a majorette, and holds membership on the Monitorial Staff Beautification Committee and International Relations Club. Linda favorite pastime is dancing. She hopes to become a social worker.

"By this we know that we love the children of God, when we love God, and keep his commandments," 1 John 5:2.

Testimonial

"Humanitarian"

Children are a gift from the Lord. Nellie Brown was employed at a young age at a mental retardation facility for children. Shortly after, since she showed strong work ethics, dedication, and commitment, she earned a position as supervisor. She was loyal to promoting the welfare of the children, ensuring employee rules and regulations were implemented against abuse or any sort of unacceptable, inappropriate behavior.

Whenever a child died at the facility and the family did not claim the body, there was no designated place to bury the child. So, children were buried in the woods or wherever space was located. Nellie was motivated to go beyond her occupational duties to rectify this situation and saw to it that there was a complete funeral service and burial on the mental retardation facility grounds for the children who passed away. She strongly felt the children deserved a respectful home going. With Nellie's leadership abilities and strong mind, she became the voice for the innocent children. Her goal was to achieve a cemetery, but her colleagues were opposed to the idea, saying it was not her responsibility. Regardless of their opposition,

Nellie was not deterred from pursuing her goal. Walking in faith, she is constantly giving her time and her gifts to serving God's people.

With time and effort, her pursuit of a dignified burial was achieved. Nellie L. Brown is now the founder of the cemetery for the mentally retarded children in the state. Her devotion to the children continued for over 40 years until her retirement.

In her retirement years, Ms. N. Brown continues to demonstrate compassion and love toward mankind as she cuddles babies that have cancer when she visits hospitals. Nellie serves on the outreach ministry and feeds the homeless at her church, Saint Martin De Porres Church, where she has been an active member for over 50 years. Ms. Nellie Brown has always been positive and spiritually energetic.

"For the Lord is good; his mercy is everlasting; and his truth endureth to all generations," Psalm 100:5.

Testimonial

"First Cousins Reunion"

Our family is grateful for the union of Mr. and Mrs. Timothy Brown who raised nine daughters and two sons from a relationship of love, faith, unity, and excellent work ethics.

My mother and her siblings planted seeds of fruits into their children's lives, seeds that blossomed from the generations that include: pastors, teachers, principals, entrepreneurs, counselors, managers, gardeners, military workers, postal workers, security workers, food caterer, fire chief, professionals, deacons, and administrators.

Work ethics have always been a vital part of our family roots. We grew up as a very closely knitted family, dedicated to providing for all family members. While many of us moved from our hometown to reach our destiny and fulfill our dreams, some, depending on our schedule, would return home for the annual "First Cousins" reunions.

It was after our auntie's funeral when two cousins and I discussed having a "First Cousins" reunion annually at Easter time. So this started the foundation of the reunion at Easter in 2000. Each year, cousins come from New York, California, Maryland, and Washington, D.C., to our hometown in Columbia, South Carolina, to fellowship. This 3-day reunion is planned with fun-filled festivities. We kick off Fridays with a fish fry, enjoy a planned field trip on Saturdays, and church on Sunday mornings, culminating with a festive banquet Sunday evening.

Each year I love seeing my family and celebrating with fun, food, and fellowship. We laugh, embrace all the love for one another, and thank God for the blessings He bestows.

"These things I have spoken unto you, that in me ye might have peace. In the world ye shall have tribulation: but be of good cheer; I have overcome the world," John 16:33.

Testimonial

"Family Tribulation"

Auntie Irmer, Uncle Ted, and their daughter Veronica always welcomed me into their home during my summer vacations. I enjoyed watching the livestock which I didn't see on a regular basis growing up in my hometown. Auntie Irmer was a longtime, faithful servant of the Lord at the family church, and she knew how to win the battle against spiritual attacks.

Their daughter grew into a young adult, got married, and gave birth to a lovely baby girl whom they named Dana. She grew up in the family church also and joined the choir. When Dana started her family, her little ones grew up in the church as well. One day as she was driving home from church choir rehearsal, another driver lost control of the car and slammed into her car, resulting in serious life-threatening injuries to her. She was hospitalized and comatose for months.

Dana's mother, auntie, and saints of their family church were in constant prayers for her healing and complete recovery. Her mother and grandmother took turns regularly at the hospital to support and inspire her to fight back for her life. The Lord answered the prayers of the righteous. She awakened from her coma and began her long road toward rehabilitation. She had to learn to walk, talk, and use her muscles again, but she fought back like a true soldier of Christ the King.

With the Lord's healing power and the provision of her mother's gift of medical expertise, she received what she needed to recover. Her mom, Veronica, has always been a strong warrior for the Lord. Her tough love in her daughter's rehab contributed to the successful healing.

After she was discharged from the hospital, she lived at her mother's home for continued care. After a year of God's grace and her mom's and grandmom's prayers, she started the recovery process and was able to successfully raise her three young children. Today, Dana is fully recovered and living a normal life. She has her own home, drives her own car, and is singing praises with the choir once again.

Praise the Lord for the healing. Christians are not exempt from tribulations due to living in a fallen world. Our faith in God gets tested. Yet, we absolutely must trust the Lord to guide our steps through all of life's crises.

"Let the redeemed of the Lord say so, whom he hath redeemed from the hand of the enemy," Psalm 107:2.

Testimonial

"Protection of God"

Being employed at a state correctional institution for 4 years as secretary for the chief psychiatrist was, at times, a very challenging job for me. I scheduled inmate appointments for office visitation and prescription refills.

This was a maximum security facility that housed 2,000 inmates. I was never fearful of harm or danger because I knew the Lord was my protector. But it did not prevent me from being tested. I arrived at my desk one day to find a personal letter from an inmate promising me protection from other inmates if I would consent to his instructions. This letter was so demonic I dropped it like "a hot potato." I also failed to notify the authorities.

At lunchtime, I requested to be escorted out of the building for security purposes. When I returned from lunch, I was asked to meet with the warden as the secretary had found the letter and reported the incident. I was admonished for not reporting the letter the inmate had given me. Then the warden asked if I had reservations about continuing to work in that location. I responded no, as I was determined not to allow Satan to remove me from my place of employment.

It is the Lord who has protected me all of my life, and I want to walk like I am being protected by an Almighty God, always glorifying His name.

"And he said, Hearken ye, all Judah, and ye inhabitants of Jerusalem, and thou king Jehoshaphat, Thus saith the Lord unto you, Be not afraid nor dismayed by reason of this great multitude; for the battle is not yours, but God's," 2 Chronicles 20:15.

Testimonial

"Protection of God from Peeping Tom"

Working after school enabled me to cover my senior dues and expenses for my graduation cap, gown, prom attendance, and senior pictures. I did not earn enough money to afford a car, so I had to rely on public transportation to get home after work. On a rainy, cold night at the bus stop, it was hard to resist a neighbor's offer to drive me home. I didn't know much about my neighbor Sam, except he seemed to have been friendly, was a bachelor, and lived a few blocks from our family home. Sam offer to drive me home from work once in a while and I would accept the ride home.

After I graduated from high school, I attended a trade school and worked as a secretary at a state agency. Finally, I was able to purchase a car for transportation to and from work.

Part of my maturity was to learn that "nothing is free." My neighbor Sam was actually not the "nice neighbor" that he initially portrayed himself to be. Sam was as slick and subtle as a snake. For 2 years, he harassed me, pouring paint over my car and slashing my tires. A year later, he set my car on fire. Sam would always perform these evil acts during the nighttime when everyone was asleep, and in a court of law, a person has to actually witness a criminal act before she make any accusations against the perpetrator.

One night Sam came to my home and shined a flashlight through the bedroom window, and, of course, I witnessed this act. I hired an attorney and pressed charges for "Peeping Tom and trespassing." The law for "Peeping Tom" states the victim's body has to be in the room. I could not shoot him, because the law states the perpetrator has to come inside the home to make that legal. So, we could only press charges for trespassing on private property.

While Sam never came on my property after going to court, the harassment did not completely stop. Late one night as I was driving to my auntie's home, I noticed a car parked a block from my home. As I approached the car, the lights were turned off and the car backed up. As this movement drew my attention, I looked into the car . . . and saw Sam.

Shortly after this incident, I moved to California. I thank God this battle was not mine, and I thank God for protecting me.

"And the Lord God commanded the man, saying, Of every tree of the garden thou mayest freely eat. But of the tree of the knowledge of good and evil, thou shalt not eat of it: for in the day that thou eatest thereof thou shalt surely die," Genesis 2:16–17.

Testimonial

"Warnings"

Warnings inform us in advance of danger to eliminate the consequences from it. Adam and Eve were warned about the forbidden tree; God commanded them not to eat from this tree. We inherited their sinful nature, and thus, consequences of their disobedience, including death.

Our high school band director would always warn the band members to leave the visiting team's concession stands at the beginning of the fourth quarter during the football game for our safety. Mr. Jacobs, our band director, would observe students from the rivalry school congregating in large numbers around the arena where our band was seated. Because our football team was winning the game, the rivalry schools would often pose threats to our band. Of course, we followed Mr. Jacobs's instructions and remained safe during all our band field trips.

During the week of orientation upon my employment at the United States Postal Service (USPS), warnings against theft and dishonesty were emphasized. This was mandatory because the job description required handling millions of valuables sent by the public. Orientation was a time to come clean concerning any individual's previous criminal charges or past incidents with the law. Everyone was warned that a personal background investigation would be held on each individual. If any criminal or unethical findings resulted from this background check, that person would be terminated.

Warnings can also notify or suggest something to a person. I recall one day when the Lord notified me that my mother would be in heaven within 1 year, so I immediately traveled to my hometown to relocate where my mother was currently residing to spend quality time with her for the duration of her life. Having the opportunity to help my sisters and other family members who were taking care of my mother was a blessing, and I am grateful to God for the warning. About 6 months after my relocation with my mom, my mother went to be with Lord, as He had revealed to me. I miss her, but know I will see her again and am glad to have spent time with her during her last days on earth.

Jesus has warned us about Satan, hell, and salvation. Where are you planning to spend *your* eternity? Jesus is waiting for you. Come as you are. He will cleanse you and make you brand-new. Accept Christ as your personal Savior this day and free yourself from the bondage of sin; heaven will rejoice and be your eternal destiny.

"Death and life are in the power of the tongue: and they that love it shall eat the fruit thereof," Proverbs 18:21.

Testimonial

"Power of the Tongue"

For years I suffered with a sore throat, always in September. I used to say, "Oh, September is near. My throat will be sore, and I cannot eat or swallow." I was unaware that I was speaking the illness into existence. My prayer partner reminded me about the power of the tongue. Afterward, I started saying, "I will never have another sore throat at any time." I give God the glory, as I have not had a sore throat in 18 years!

There was a man named Chris. He wanted time off from work and decided to play a joke. He called to the attendance office at the post office and told the clerk Chris was deceased. Two years later, Chris was murdered. God's Word is true. With his tongue, Chris spoke his death.

When I was only 3 years old, I told my auntie that I would be moving to California and buying a car. Today, I live in Los Angeles, California, and I own a car. These words were spoken as a baby; yet, 25 years later, they came to pass.

My sister Gloria and her husband were anticipating buying their dream home. She gathered boxes and started packing their personal belongings before the approval for the house. It was an act of faith and works for with her tongue she gratefully praised God for the home. Months later the couple and their two children were living in and enjoying their dream home.

Use the power of your tongue today to make a difference in your life. Start a personal relationship with Jesus. Tell Him all your troubles and accept Him as your Savior. Jesus said: "For by thy words thou shalt be justified, and by thy words thou shalt be condemned," Matthew 12:37.

"To every thing there is a season, and a time to every purpose under the heaven," Ecclesiastes 3:1.

Testimonial

"A Time to Every Purpose"

Time and season are essential to our livelihood. Yearly we have seasonal weather: winter, spring, summer, and fall. In sports, there is football, basketball, baseball, and golf played in their time and season. Peaches, plums, watermelons, and strawberries are grown in their appointed time.

I had a zeal for work as a teenager. Whenever an opportunity arose to perform a job alongside a family member, I was ready. Wanting to earn money to purchase what I wanted or needed motivated me. In my life I learned there is a purpose, season, and time for me to work and that money does not grow on trees.

After working over the years, I am in the season in time to leave my secular job and serve the Lord full time. I will continue to be planted in the house of the Lord and bring forth fruit for the rest of my life.

There is a time to keep silent. When I am instructed to work an assignment, I have no problem performing that assignment. I have enjoyed working various jobs and have always respected managerial personnel. Life has taught me no place of employment is perfect because we are not perfect people. So, I have always respected my work environment. But I have trusted the Lord's time and purpose for all my employment jobs, issues, and am witness: "He will work it out in His time."

There is a time to speak. If I am instructed this season to perform an assignment that is not in my job description, I may ask, "Do I have the ability to perform the task? Do the tasks call for unethical behavior? Have instructions and resources been provided?" And by taking the time to speak about these concerns, management will assess the situation and provide necessary resources to perform the assignment.

There is a time for Jesus to return to earth, yet no one knows the exact time. So why you have time, make this your season to start a relationship with Jesus Christ, and be ready for His return.

"Notwithstanding the Lord stood with me, and strengthened me; that by me the preaching might be fully known, and that all the Gentiles might hear: and I was delivered out of the mouth of the lion," 2 Timothy 4:17.

Testimonial

"Called to Preach"

My cousin Joe made a few bad choices and was headed down the road of destruction. As a preteen, he could not discern the tricks and traps of Satan. For a few years, he was living out of God's will in bondage to things of the world.

His mother is a prayer warrior and trusted the Lord for deliverance. She was in constant prayer, pleading the blood of Jesus on his life and pleading for the Lord to use him as He wishes.

Yes, the Lord answered all of her prayers. The enemy tried to take Joe's life, but God protected him, placed Joe's feet on a solid rock, and established his comings and goings.

Today, Joe has his bachelor's of art, and two masters' of arts degrees. He is the pastor of a church in the Chicago area and married with one daughter and one son. Joe heard the voice of the Lord and answered "yes" to His will and His way.

Joe has been a blessing to his mother, ensuring her comfort and basic needs in purchasing her a new home and a new car. Like Joe, the Lord is calling us into His Kingdom and He wants to use us, too. We might be saying, "Lord, I've messed up big time, feel awful, and am not worthy of you." But God's hands are reaching out to the unsaved person always, saying, "Come, my child; I forgive you of all unrighteousness."

At times we think we are at the end of the rope and ready to throw in the towel. Just remember, God is calling you: "Come to Jesus." We may have backslid and tried to clean up our own act. Only Jesus can cleanse you and make you whole. He did it for my cousin Joe, and He will do it for you. Come to Jesus!

"Surely goodness and mercy shall follow me all the days of my life: and I will dwell in the house of the Lord forever," Psalm 23:6.

Testimonial

"Promises Fulfilled"

God promises to supply all my needs through Christ. Let me clarify, He will supply all your *needs,* not your *wants.* I may want a house on the ocean and a Mercedes-Benz. But what I need is a roof over my head, and my God will supply my home. What I need is transportation to get to work, church, and essential places. My God will supply a car for those purposes.

There was a time I needed somewhere to live and could not afford to rent an apartment or home by myself. I had never rented a room from a family or individual, but know there is a "first time" for anything in this life. So I did some research on the possibility of renting from a homeowner, interviewed with this lady, and later signed an agreement to occupy one room in her home with shared kitchen, bathroom, and other room privileges.

After renting the room for 2 years, I was ready for my own space and freedom. The homeowner was a very nice Christian lady who welcomed me and made me feel at home. Having a place to stay at this time in my life was a real need, but my finances were challenged. While living in this lady's home, my place of employment was conveniently located only 6 miles from her residence.

However, during the fourth year of renting I began my plan to move out. I started fasting and praying unto the Lord. I would say to God, "Lord, I don't know how you are going to work this out, but you promised." I then started walking by faith, packing things into boxes, throwing away junk that I did not need. I contacted my real estate agent and started searching for places to buy. The real estate market was down, so I felt this was an opportunistic time to purchase a home.

Whatever God promises, He has the power to perform it . . . and He did. I was blessed with the finances to purchase a condo only 3 miles from my place of employment. And even better, the mortgage note was *half* of what I was paying for rent. Alleluia!

Hours before I was awarded the bid from this foreclosure property, the sale price dropped an additional $8,000. At that moment, I knew the condo was mine. Months earlier, the Lord revealed in my dream that I would be moving from the lady's home. God knew my need, and He did as He promised. You may not want Christ in your life, but believe me—you *need* Jesus Christ in your life. You were created by Him, for Him, and you shall receive the promises through Him.

Testimonial

"Promises Fulfilled"

In writing this book, I am in the season to testify of God's goodness and mercy that have followed me all the days of my life, only because of how great our God is, not because I deserve it; for, I am a sinner saved by grace.

I was pregnant out of His will. Yet, God did not forsake me, but extended goodness and mercy to answer prayers. The prayers of forgiveness I received from my Lord; and bonus, my prayer for a beautiful, healthy baby girl was answered. My daughter, Tanta T. Brown was born.

I was in the valley of heartaches and pain, and Satan had a stronghold on me. But I trusted in the Lord and His promises. God has never left nor forsaken me. Because of His mercies and loving-kindness, the Good Shepherd leads me through the valley. The power of Jesus healed my broken heart from a hurtful relationship and broke the stronghold of Satan . . . and now I am free. The truth will set you free!

He showed mercy in the sins of my youth. During our younger years, my cousins, brothers, sisters, and I would engage in rock fights with neighboring youth. During one of these rock-fighting incidents, a young girl sitting on the brick wall, talking to her friend, was innocently struck in the head. She had to receive stitches in her head and made me think, this could have been fatal. As I was the eldest, the so-called ringleader, I felt responsible for this incident. I was very hurt, sad, and remorseful. I praise the Lord the young girl did not die. She recovered and resumed her normal life activities.

My life has been crowned with goodness and mercy. My soul cries out, and I shout praises to His holy name, "The Lord is good, and His mercy is everlasting."

Testimonial

"Promises Fulfilled"

I have trusted the Lord, and He has kept His promise all of my life. He said, "No weapon formed against me shall prosper and the battle is His." God has fought many battles for me. God has directed me to the path not to be ignorant of Satan's devices. Because we wrestle not against flesh and blood but against principalities, powers, and rulers of darkness and spiritual wickedness in high places, we have to trust our battles to God.

The Lord directed me down a path of protection when I was 16 years old. During one period in my life, I worked serving salad in a restaurant at a large hotel after my school day ended. Upon leaving school, I would ride the city bus to work, and then home. I did not feel safe at night walking a few miles from the bus stop to my house. I asked my brother George Edward to meet me at the bus stop on this one particular night because a murderer was on the loose, according to the news.

Once I arrived at the bus stop this particular night, my brother was not there. So as I began walking home, I felt like I was in the midst of a horror movie. Two remaining blocks to get home, I began to feel the cold wind blowing stronger, the trees whistling louder, and sky seemed darker than ever. No one was around; no cars were on the street. As I was walking, my thoughts of my brother disappointed me. I told myself, if I make it home, I am going to wring his neck off like a chicken.

When I finally made it home safely and ran upstairs to George Edward's room, my heart was touched. He was sound asleep, and I realized he had good intentions but could not stay awake to meet me. I then silently closed his door and did not disturb his rest. I realized it is better to trust in the Lord and not man: for He will direct your path to peace.

Testimonial

"Promises Fulfilled"

There was a time when I attended church and did not tithe. I gave whatever money was in my purse. My goal was to put something in the plate. Financially, tithing was not affordable in my mind and the Lord knew my heart.

It was on a Sunday service that the church was really on fire. The Holy Spirit was heavy on the saints. I enjoyed the Spirit so much, I was convicted of tithing. All this joy was in the house of the Lord. Tithing, not the government, supports and aids the church's financial responsibilities. When I enter the church from the hot or cold weather, I feel cool air or heat inside. These and other bills are why we need to obey God's commandments that come with promises: to tithe.

After that service, I started tithing and giving offerings faithfully. I sacrificed a couple of bills to pay my tithes. A few years into tithing, the windows of heaven were opened and I received blessings. In 2005, my condo sold to the first buyer seeking to purchase it, and I received a hefty profit. I was then able to obtain my dream home and pay off my credit card debt, all because of my faithful tithing and additional offerings in obedience to His Word.

Be a cheerful giver unto the Lord's storehouse!

Testimonial

"Promises Fulfilled"

The Lord has never left nor forsaken me. No matter what the circumstances, I knew He was there for me. When the enemy attacks, Jesus is there to give me the victory.

Since really knowing the Lord, I have always trusted in His promises and never feared. On one particular night I was confronted with evil. After a hard day's work, I wanted to get home and relax. While driving home, I noticed two cars parked diagonally in each lane. I immediately discerned trouble. A roadblock by civilians was a setup, inflicting fear and harm among innocent people. Being the first person in this roadblock, my car was next to the troublemakers who were facilitating the roadblock. It was approximately 12:30 A.M. in the Los Angeles airport area and traffic was backed up in this area due to late-night arrivals.

No car could move in any direction; traffic was halted by these troublemakers. But my God gave me instructions how to proceed out of Satan's so-called roadblock. Because God had placed me first in the lineup of halted cars next to the troublemakers, God positioned me to break the ill-intended plans and barriers of these satanic individuals. I was led by the Holy Spirit to check for cars coming in the opposite direction. It was safe, so I proceeded to go around the blocked car. As I drove into the opposite lane, trying to get away from this evil person who was causing the roadblock, he also moved his car to block me from proceeding. But God had a plan in this moving also. Once the troublemaker moved to block me, an opening was created for the other cars to go around the roadblock and traffic started moving clear of any roadblocks and was normal once again. This move was clearly of God to destroy the plan of the enemy.

I remained calm while being led by the Lord through this 20-minute ordeal, knowing that the Lord had never left nor forsaken me. Trust Him as your Savior: He will never leave nor forsake you. Praise God!